THE ANGLES OF LIGHT

Also by Luci Shaw:

Friends for the Journey, with Madeleine L'Engle

God in the Dark

Horizons

LifePath

Listen to the Green

Polishing the Petoskey Stone

Postcard from the Shore

A Prayer Book for Spiritual Friends, with Madeleine L'Engle

The Risk of Birth, anthology

The Secret Trees

The Sighting

Sightseers into Pilgrims, anthology

The Swiftly Tilting Worlds of Madeleine L'Engle, festschrift

Water My Soul

A Widening Light, anthology

WinterSong: Christmas Readings, with Madeleine L'Engle

Writing the River

The Angles of Light

new & selected poems

Luci Shaw

HAROLD
SHAW
PUBLISHERS

Wheaton, Illinois

Grateful acknowledgment is made to the periodicals and collections in which these poems, some in slightly different form, first appeared:

The Bellingham Herald, The Christian Century, Christianity & Literature, Christianity & the Arts, Cornerstone, Crux, First Things, Image, Inklings, Kinesis, Leadership Journal, Mars Hill Review, Procreation, Radix, The Sow's Ear Review, Wheaton Alumni, Wrestlings

"Advent visitation," "The door, the window," "Frosty," "The labors of angels," "Snow fall," "White on black," and "Winter nights" appeared in *WinterSong: Christmas Readings* (with Madeleine L'Engle), © 1996 by Harold Shaw Publishers. Used by permission.

"Teresa Speaks to God" appeared in *Prisms of the Soul,* Marcy Darin, Ed., Morehouse Publishing, 1997. Used by permission of the author.

"The Holiness of Iona" appeared in *Friends for the Journey,* © 1997 by Luci Shaw and Madeleine L'Engle. Published by Servant Publications, Box 8617, Ann Arbor, Michigan, 48107. Used with permission.

"Rising: The Underground Tree" appeared in *The Best Spiritual Writing 1998,* edited by Philip Zaleski, © 1998, HarperCollins. Used by permission of the author.

"Some mornings she simply cannot" appeared in *The Best Spiritual Writing 1999,* edited by Philip Zaleski, © 1999, HarperCollins. Used by permission of the author.

We have sought to secure permissions for all copyrighted material in this book. Where acknowledgment was inadvertently omitted, the publisher expresses regret.

Published in association with the literary agency of Alive Communications, Inc., 1465 Kelly Johnson Blvd., Suite 320, Colorado Springs, CO 80920.

ISBN 0-87788-0212

Cover design by Kathy Lay Burrows
Cover photo by Luci Shaw

Library of Congress Cataloging-in-Publication Data

Shaw, Luci
    The angles of light : new and selected poems / by Luci Shaw.
       p. cm.
    ISBN 0-87788-021-2
    Title.

    PS3569.H384 A84 2000
    811'.54—dc21   99-051752

06 05 04 03 02 01 00
10 9 8 7 6 5 4 3 · 2 1

To Karen Cooper

Contents

Introduction

How to Enter a Poem

Picture a bridge built from one side of a river to another. The engineers have constructed it from both ends, planning for it to join in the middle. The two ends of the bridge must meet if the traffic is to cross it in both directions.

In the poem the writer has made a bridge, or half a bridge, across the watery expanse of understanding. The half-structure reaches toward your imagination from the poet's side. In order to join it, you, the reader, must extend the other half of the bridge from your side of the riverbank. You must take the risk of reaching toward the constructed work the poet offers you, and in meeting it, join it, so that the images, ideas, emotions, perceptions, music, and rhythm can flow from the poet's mind into your own.

On an occasion such as a poetry reading, your listening and your focused response flow back to the poet across the bridge you two have just built—a two-way communication. James Dickey said once, "Don't let the poet write down to you; read up, listen up to him. Reach for him from your gut; the heart and mind will come into it too."

Several years ago a student of mine, Syida Long, wrote a poem that starts like this:

> *Enter a poem from the inside*
> *like a bridge stanchion*
> *through fog . . .*

Syida is from San Francisco, and she had in mind the drive across the Bay Bridge, which is sometimes choked in fog. Her image suggests some of the risks of entering a poem. It's a journey into someone else's mind, into the unknown, into mystery. But as you move forward into it line by line (the way you'd drive onto the Bay Bridge yard by yard), the way opens up, becomes clear, and the structure holds firm under you despite the feeling that you are entering a cloud. When you reach the other side, you will know that the bridge of the poem has held you and led you into the poet's mind, experience, and emotion.

For this to happen most effectively, you may want to read the poem aloud, and let its rhythm and the resonant music of its language enter your ear as the words penetrate your eye and the ideas and images reach your mind. This will vastly aid your comprehension of the poem. Read it aloud again. And again. Each time you read it, it will open itself up—make itself more accessible and vivid to you.

As we read the poem, we realize that the beat or the rhythm of much of today's poetry is governed by body pulses (the heartbeat, the breathing rhythm, the walking rate) more than the arbitrary patterns of a formal poem such as a sonnet or a villanelle. Reading the work aloud allows us to participate in these natural rhythms, which will inform us subliminally; as we feel where the beat comes in the lines, we will discover clues to the mood and context of the writer.

Your reading of, or your listening to, a poem is a creative exercise, almost as creative as the writing of it. Each individual comes to a poem with a unique, personal frame of reference, a set of experiences unlike anyone else's, so that even universals, the easily recognizable images and ideas common to most of us, will have a distinct cast and color unique to your mind, and different from the writer's. Because a skillful poem often suggests rather than explains, there may be some enigmatic gaps, some silences, some breaks in logic, which you will fill in from your own imagination, your own set of kaleidoscopic impressions. As you read a poem, you too are creating, forming something unique and meaningful in your mind out of someone else's words.

A poem is as different from descriptive or expository prose as singing or whistling is from talking. You must come to poetry with a different set of expectations than you would with a sermon on the raising of Lazarus, or a lecture on apartheid, or a talk on how to help a friend with terminal illness. Where most prose gives us information or instruction, poetry offers reflection on something *wonder*-full, some event or phenomenon that has caused the poet to express wonder in a way that draws the reader into the wonderful as well. Christopher Fry said: "Poetry is the language by which man explores his own amazement."

But a poem rarely attempts to tell a whole story. It's not like a speech with an introduction, four points, a summary, and a conclusion. While a poem has a beginning, middle, and end, it is more like a small fragment of experience viewed close up. It hints, suggests, touches, probes, without preaching or pushing too hard. Poems are packed with sounds and pictures—the doorways to the inner life of objects, experiences, relationships—the stuff of the extraordinary ordinary.

William Stafford has said: "Language is a great river of possibilities swirling around us all the time." The poet's job is to choose words like tumblers of water from this river of language, and match them up with the details of a poetic image. As a reader, learn to latch onto the concrete details of a poem—the pegs from which it hangs, the particulars that give it grit and authenticity.

You will want, also, to discover what the poem is *about,* at a more philosophical level. Often this is couched in metaphor, which is in the business of comparison, or carrying over meaning from one arena of experience to another. (Even the word *metaphor* means to transport or to carry over. I recently learned with astonishment that the modern Greek word for moving van is *metaphoros!*)

An example of metaphor: "The ship plows the sea." The image of a farmer's plow slicing and turning the soil of a wide field, throwing up behind it a furrow of glistening soil, brings to mind the way a ship cuts through the fluid surface of the ocean, leaving a wake of waves. Though the two images are similar (which makes the metaphor possible), they are also unlike, and there is as much meaning to be found in the unlikeness as in the likeness.

There's mystery here. We all long to find meaning in our lives, and a poem mysteriously helps us to make the connections, to pull things together, to shine light on things from a fresh, surprising angle and thus create a richer, larger picture from the small brush strokes of specific detail. We create a significance.

As you enter a poem you will need to *feel* and *see* it as well as to listen to it and analyze it critically. Robert Bly has said, "The eye reports to the brain, the ear to the heart, so don't listen to poetry just with your head." Poetry is not irrational, but it arises from the logic of the imagination and the senses rather than from the purely linear, rational kind of thought.

Practice a kind of relaxed concentration. Take time. Breathe deeply. Flow with the lines of words, and bridge your way into each poem with your ears, and your skin, and your nose, and your eyes, and even your tongue. See the word pictures. Pretend your mind is a projection screen on which the poet is shining a series of images. They're called "poems."

—*Luci Shaw*

1

WE KNOW THIS TO START WITH

We know this to start with:

If we understood everything we wouldn't
be baffled. But mystery lives; somehow
without witchcraft or chicanery

we collect sounds and colors in a skyward
dish, like fruit in a bowl, and channel them
into verisimilitude—faces talking at us

from the tube's glass eye. Hallways of fog
enfold us in enigma. And then, the marvel of
window glass—how can anything be

hard enough to stop the hand and
hold its smudge while letting through this
soft light? The one wheat kernel that

breeds a thousand—a miracle of
loaves over and over again.
The stars, invisible in the blind day

revealed, thick as pollen, by the absence
of light. A billion spiky grass blades that melt
into a perfectly flat horizon. The Holy Ghost

waking me in my bedroom, drenching my
dry heart with fluid syllables, breathing
flesh onto the fetal bones of this poem.

Litchfield Woods: Believing the light
May 1999

When I think of those woods, I think a basket
filling up with morning as it pours
over the lip of the mountains. Also I remember the way
the noon light falls between the saplings' vertical
pencil strokes, turning each young leaf, in its

brash green, into a lens to scatter bright lumens
like foil over bark and blade. The maple leaves
believe in the light with foliate faith. They dream it
all night long, and angle their faces to meet morning.
And on overcast, enigmatic days,

light's blessing still filters down, even in
the beginnings of storm. Or in a sun shower,
that gentle golden drizzle—sundrops condensed
and falling—wetting the leaves to a shine
and dripping from them to the soaked forest floor.

Speckled toads, camouflaged the color of humus,
breathe light in. Birds swim it, fleeter than fish.
Buttercups open their mouths to it,
believing that when their petals fall
they will become pieces of sky.

Light makes even the dirt blossom—watch
for these signatures of spring: the up-curling fiddleheads,
the purple bleed of the wild phlox along the ditches,
the way the bee comes to the tongue of the lupine
for its surfeit of sweetness.

Rising: The underground tree

(Cornus sanguinea and *cornus canadensis)*

One spring in Tennessee I walked a tunnel
under dogwood trees, noting the petals
(in fours like crosses) and at each tender apex
four russet stains dark as Christ-wounds.
I knew that with the year the dogwood flower heads
would ripen into berry clusters bright as drops of gore.

Last week, a double-click on Botany
startled me with the kinship of those trees
and bunch-berries, whose densely crowded mat
carpets the deep woods around my valley cabin.
Only their flowers—those white quartets of petals—
suggest the blood relationship. Since then I see

the miniature leaves and buds as tips of trees
burgeoning underground, knotted roots like limbs
pushing up to light through rock and humus.
The pure cross-flowers at my feet redeem
their long, dark burial in the ground, show how even
a weight of stony soil cannot keep Easter at bay.

Folio

Flattened like coins on train tracks
the prunus leaves unfurl along their twigs
in copper ovals. She bends down,
peers in. Shadowed underneath,
each leaf greens in its
charcoal dark, laced with veins
rosy as human arterial blood, delicate
as her own most minor capillaries.

Here are two secrets: the bud
bursting pink from the groin where
leaf stem embraces branch; the curled worm
slung in its pale cocoon, waiting.

Here is another: she has walked around
all day, feeling raw as that bloody leaf,
or worse, a blank page. Priceless
as a flat penny, she'll end up
shriveled for sure, food for the worm.
Against the odds, maybe she'll bloom first.

Magnificat

I am singing my Advent to you, God: How all year
I've felt your thrusts, every sound and sight piercing
like a little sword—the creak of gulls, the racket
as waves jostle pebbles, the road after rain—
shining like a river, the scrub of wind on the cheek, a flute
trilling—clean as a knife, the immeasurable chants of green,
of sky: messages, announcements. But of what? Who?

Then last Tuesday, one peacock feather (surprise!)
spoke from the grass; Flannery called hers "a genuine
word of the Lord." And I—as startled as Mary, nearly,
at your arrival in her chamber (the invisible
suddenly seen, urgent, iridescent, having put on light
for her regard)—I brim over like her, quickening. I can't
stop singing, thoroughly pregnant with Word!

At the edge

A conspiracy of secrets seems
    to join my open eye and
        the satin gaze of a pond

that returns my glance without
    a ripple, a blink. A dialog
        of sorts. Mirror images

that only darkly hint at what
    lies below. But that magnetic
        blue of iris . . .

The pupil at the center is
    the one deep keyhole to the mind
        of water or watcher.

Under the skin of light our mysteries
    remain unfathomable.
        With eyes wide

we both know how to safeguard secrets.
    But night closes in and burns them, green
        and purple, into our dreams.

Bubble

I watch it being blown, swelling and rising
from my grandson's red plastic ring, fresh-filled
with eager air, tenuous as just-spilled
dandelion silk, a fluid wobble, quite surprising

me with its likeness to our cosmic bubble,
all greens and blues, each continent and sea
etched in bright enamel by God and gravity—
a film's fine iridescence fixed. The trouble

is: before the shivering, frail balloon has hovered
long it bursts in a star of spray that pricks my skin
with cool fireworks, so that, in vanishing, it winks
at my comparison just as the simile is offered.

But mind's a watercolor paper. This visual spasm
has brushed me with its indelible, swift
rainbow strokes of form and gleam. My visions shift
between the micro- and the macrocosm,

ephemeral both, as radiant as grace,
glass globules in the furnace air, both sealed
off after a creative breath, and then annealed,
floating their minor vessels into space.

Puzzle: Tuolumne River

Just now, a yellow leaf the shape of an eye
flying, settling on glacial rock, watching us;

the river, spilling its slow snow-melt, conserving
its ancient secrets, its questions;

each hour a new riddle showing: the way water, in
its softness, knuckles holes in granite;

the sun's burn across ripples, crowding
the chill olive of shadow; the wedlock

of moss with pine root; your cascade's
cursive eloquence that drowns my mineral hush.

Managing God

2 Samuel 6:1-23
for Eugene Peterson

A stumble of beasts, a lurch
of the oxcart, and Uzzah's hands leap
to harness God's holy box. On the instant
he feels heaven's fire strike—
an unmanageable current flares
to the ends of his bones,
sizzles his grasp to ash.

David, rising as the same perilous
burn ignites his fingers and
his flying feet, self-abandoned, his
spirit blazing, is stripped naked by joy
to servant girls, himself, and God,
who plays him like a wind-harp.

From her arrogant window Michal's jealousy
watches this wanton worship—holiness dancing
beyond propriety. Snuffing David's joy
like a candle, she learns the swiftness
of Yahweh; irony has neutered her fecundity;
contempt has cauterized her womb.

"Total recall"

they call it. Like an aura
orbiting his head
life printed itself on him
so that with a mere twitch of neurons
he could deliver all detail

into the present. He'd recall
with sensuous precision the belch and
roar of a London bus, the oily gutter
mud, the shape of a dragonfly darting
over lilies at Kew. A chestnut

freshly brought forth from its
spiky green shell. The word *retina*.
The sound of a door shut softly
far back in childhood.
His left hemisphere

was inscribed with
the dates of the kings and queens
of England—fragments most of us
shed like epithelial cells
in a daily divestment

to free new space in the brain.
His memory, known to be an asset
for scholarly research,
he found intolerable for life. Who
would lust for the clutter
of all those marching minutes,
the trivia of an infinite number
of days? In the end the smothered mind
took the body with it, and the thick
air around him clarified suddenly.

What secret purple wisdom
Wedding poem for Jeff & Donna

What word informs the world,
and moves the worm along in his blind tunnel?

What secret purple wisdom tells the iris edges
to unfold in frills? What juiced and emerald thrill

urges the sap until the bud resolves
its tight riddle? What irresistible command

unfurls this cloud above *this* greening hill,
or one more wave—its spreading foam and foil—

across the flats of sand? What minor thrust
of energy issues up from humus in a froth

of ferns? Delicate as a laser, it filigrees
the snow, the stars. Listen close—What silver sound

thaws winter into spring? Speaks clamor into singing?
Gives love for loneliness? It is this

unterrestrial pulse, deep as heaven, that folds you
in its tingling embrace, gongs in your echo heart.

2

THE LABORS OF ANGELS

The labors of angels

Plucking our meager treasures, grain
by grain, we disregard celestial messengers
to our jeopardy.

Sexless and muscular, angels
must wrestle, pitting light against
sinew and darkness. They arrive
without notice, blazing, terrifying us
with good news.

Barren or virgin
we bear our improbable children,
and angels raise heaven like a song.
Still, angels can weep;
in your mind's eye, see
their clear, mineral tears.

Against the indigo sky,
where judgment pulses
like an aneurysm, sunlight spins
its horizontal threads across the field until
the yellows in the standing wheat stalks
match the low light. Harvester angels
cast huge wings of shadow,
scything a crop, lifting it
from the skin of an acre
like fleece from a sheep's flank.

It is only later that they delicately
unhook teasel, thistle, burdock
from the heavy gold grain.

Upon seeing the painting by Roger Wagner, The Harvest Is the
End of the World and the Reapers Are Angels

At West Beach, Lummi Island
for Kathryn Yanni

My boots crunch down the slope, clamber over
the bleached bones of trees. I conquer a tide of pebbles;
at wave edge I stoop and finger one, another,

fondling their flecks and facets, their skin soft as peaches.
Their colors burn my retina. Uninvited words leap into my
      throat.
I am astonished; from what pleat of brain tissue did they
      spring?

Schist, agate, gneiss, shale, scree, granite, quartz—they use
my lips to utter their abrasive syllables. God is in these
crystalline names, in the mineral click, the stony rattle

of gravel under the scrolling breakers. God speaks the
      language
of stones. I am a polished stone myself, and he is speaking
my name. With every ripple, every spit of rain that wets a
      pebble

into its real color, he tells me, I am washing you with salt,
I am grinding you smooth to my touch. With rain I caress
your oval shape, your apricot silk, and show you your true
      self.

St. Martin's Chapel II: Isaiah 40
Cathedral of St. John the Divine

Kneeling, suddenly I am compelled to look up.
In the right center lancet of stained glass,
in the lead-colored sky above St. Joan in flames,
a chink is missing. *Comfort, comfort my people.*
The grisaille is broken—a storm? a flung stone?
The tempest carries them off . . . and a light sharper
than the bright glass takes the shape of an eagle.
They mount up with wings . . . Air enters with the light—
arrowing into the shadows, sweeping dust
from the stonework with a fierce whisk of breath.

Listen, again. The young woman priest
with blond hair is still reading Isaiah:
He gives power to the faint. A voice says, "Cry out!"
No stake is visible, but orange tongues
lick out from Joan in a kind of nimbus.
Incredible. She is playing something—
a viola da gamba? No, it's a stylized palm branch;
she is offering it to her executioners.
The glory of the Lord shall be revealed . . .
Tell me, how should I hope to die?

Advent visitation

Even from the cabin window I sensed the wind's
contagion begin to infect the rags of leaves.
Then the alders gilded to it, obeisant, the way

angels are said to bow, covering their faces with
their wings, not solemn, as we suppose, but
possessed of a sudden, surreptitious hilarity.

When the little satin wind arrived
I felt its slide through the cracked-open door
(a wisp of prescience? a change in the weather?),

and after the small push of breath—You
entering with your air of radiant surprise,
I the astonished one.

These still December mornings
I fancy I live in a clear envelope of angels
like a cellophane womb. Or a soap bubble,

the colors drifting, curling. Outside
everything's tinted rose, grape, turquoise,
silver—the stones by the path, the skin of sun

on the pond ice, at night the aureola of
a pregnant moon, like me, iridescent,
almost full term with light.

The mockingbird

is clearly not

no scornful bone in
that feather body

nor mimic
imitating other birds
or us and our
predictable indoor tunes

the bird is
pure experiment

that riff at the end
how did it go again

yes
but opening
with two new notes

variations
inventions endless and
impromptu

quicksilver

in bed in the dark
and again
we hear birdsong

liquid improbable
sun at midnight

poet's work

the small throat's
inevitability
and surprise

Glass beach

Mendocino, California coast, January 1997

Yesterday the gift-store clerk
told us how far up the coast
to drive: "Once it was the city dump,"
she said. The surprise
when we got there—not just
the usual glints from a polished,
occasional shard, but a whole beach
of sea-glass.

Today the entire shore glitters
in the fresh light. Small, muscular ripples
rearrange the glisten of particles, hiss to the sun
here, look at this. Every wave, a quick,
inquisitive hand, turns over a new handful of
jewel pebbles for us—probing
for the rare, winking eye of cobalt,
the perfect lozenge of aqua, or bottle green,
frosted by the rub of rock, translucent
as the sea-water just now rinsing it again,
and again.

All the old discards
long gone—metals rusted away, paper, wood
shredded to nothing. Only
this shattered, sea-smoothed glass,
solid enough to survive the breakers
and turn to sapphires in our fingers.

Possess your soul in patience
Wedding poem for John & Christa

Own it. Hold your heart the way
you'd hold a live bird—your two hands
laced to latch it in, feeling
its feathery trembling, its fledgling
warmth, its faint anxieties
of protest, its heart stutter
against the palm of one hand, a fidget
in the pull of early light.

Possess it, restless, in
the finger cage of patience. Enfold
this promise with a blue sheen
on its neck, its wings a tremor
of small feathered bones
until morning widens like
a window, and God opens
your fingers and whispers, *Fly!*

Resurrection: Rocky York Islet
South Gulf Islands

Trial, error, and my blue kayak
have found me this rock shelf, curved
to fit my thighs, sun-warm as my blood.
Around me fractured coral-pink
crab carapaces and glistening scabs
of fish scales patch the lichened
sandstone; I realize
the resting place I've chosen is where
sea otters relieve themselves.

There's not enough bird or beast in me
for permanent contentment on a
barren shoal, but in this moment
quiet falls like wisdom; glitter
unfurls in my eye; words swim onto
the notebook page to deposit their
small scat in phrases like
the indigestible scales of rainbow fish,
like God raising what is dead to life.

The stringencies of sainthood

1

The giving up, and giving up, to God,
whose terrible holiness presses your head like

Christ's nimbus of thorns, inescapable as
an iron tonsure. No wonder Columba, hard-pressed,

vowed his own perpetual exile, moved from ruthless Eire
to Iona over the water, from whose high ground

his old land was just invisible. (Which is why, to fulfill
his vow when he went back, he bound clods of Ionic sod

under his footsoles and a rag across his eyes so that
never again would its green rub off on his feet or his eyeballs.)

2

A stalwart saint, stubborn St. Kevin
clung to Eire. (His presence still ghosts

over Glendalough's tilted grave markers,
and haunts, like a bird, the roofless stone house

where martyr priests were burned.)
Known to have dealt forcefully

with intrusive or amorous women, shoving them
unceremoniously into banks of nettles

or icy lakes, a disciplined gentility yet
kept his arm and hand thrust out the window

of his cell until a thrush perched there (for whom
that open palm, simply testing the outside

air for rain, signaled welcome) had built a nest,
hatched eggs, launched her young toward heaven.

3

St. Bridget, carved in stone, and resolute the way
women are, sits pious in Iona Abbey's fog-filled close,

her bowed head an icon of endurance
forever pecked by the beak of the descending dove.

. . . with those that weep

I can't tell

It's the same choked
explosive sound

the identical facial spasm
whether laughter or
a black sob
mouth wide as a windsock
or an open wound
eyes tight shut as slits in linen
chin clenched tears squeezing

out and running their little
rivers down your cliff
face onto the veined backs
of your hands

Belly laugh or howl of
anguish
I'm still not sure
still waiting to know
whether I should
laugh or cry with you

The writing on the rock
Magnetawan, Ontario

The morning opens, blue as innocence, over
a lake between granite shores, the old rocks
ribboned with intrusions of quartz.
For eons you northern stones
have spread your ancient pages for
a vermilion scribble of spores,
lichens illegible as lace, a murmur
of olive mosses spelling out
their microscopic struggles for foothold.

But where acid rain gnaws at the boulders
disease spreads its scabs, brittle as dust
under our fingers. Our gift to you—a silver rain
with a bitter bite. You give back what you can—
this delicate embroidery in black. I write
my journal notes; you draft your own slow chronicle
in a dialect of ruin. Tell me, has it healed anything
that some zealot has scrawled across your cliff face,
in white letters large and stark as death, "Jesus Saves"?

Oriental

for Robin, my daughter

Last spring we planted a small
Japanese maple. So meager and spindly,
its few leaves curving over its pencil-thin
stem like a derelict, half-open umbrella.

We could only imagine this year's
perfection, the dappled shade it would cast,
there, by the standing stone, its leaves
like little hands unfolding their rich, red

translucency, blessing the Chinese
water bowl half full of rounded beach stones,
its surface dimpled as water pours,
like music, from the bamboo spout.

3

A CHANGE IN THE WEATHER

A change in the weather

Yesterday was quite perfect. All day. She had been
so ready for perfection (a week of minor discontents
rumbling through the family, intermittent rain,
the cancellation of the writers' group just when her story
was ready for reading). Now, Saturday's renewal
brimmed in her memory, blue and endless,
the mountains cut clear against heaven, the lake
glistening like something just created, and at the close,
the sun lowering itself into its own bowl
of pure apricot, no sensational splashing all over
the clouds, but a pure burning, round
as a cardinal virtue, from the matchless west.

It was the kind of flawlessness to be printed
in memory, to be held, hidden, a gemstone
in the hand for next week when, like salt
clumping on a blue table, the clouds would
form again at the horizon to blot the sun.

Trip

Like our lives, we begin our day by
leaving shelter—the garage, and our street's
odd, ordinary familiarity. The morning traffic
crouches through a tunnel of trees
and onto the freeway, runs free
for a couple of miles, then slows,
bunches. We swing into the carpool lane,

penetrate a spaghetti of intersections,
emerge. The light behind
the East Bay hills expands, pressing the sky up,
up. Today I will begin to move across
continental space towards my daughter and
my daughter's daughters. My track

takes me through clots of airport traffic,
check-in, and the long fast walk—my morning
aerobics—out to the gate, and the wait,
and then the slope of the jetway. Wheeled bag
following me like a leashed terrier, I bump

aboard the metal bird that promises
freedom from terra firma. I inch down
the narrow aisle between metal and shoe
leather and into the tight seat.

We taxi, starting, stopping, starting again,
to the runway where the engines rev
and the bird moves faster, faster,

feeling every concrete jolt until
at last we are lifted by our own air speed

along the clear, unfettered path of air.

The pink hibiscus

In the space of a single psalm David's
emotional pendulum would often swing all the way
from lament to celebration. Was it an act of faith?
A surge of optimism? For myself, the oscillation
moves too often from doubt to faith and
back again; it's the stretch, the wide arc from soar
to swoop that disconcerts. Sometimes it seems
as if equilibrium comes only from
letting myself go numb. Then all the distress
of melancholia fades into a fugitive dream,
along with old happinesses, spurts of elation—
they dim into an echoing, indeterminate past.
Waiting for the nerves to tingle into life again.

And more of the same, even here on a
tropical vacation. But right now a flushed hibiscus,
inviting a bee to its pink lip, its swollen stamen
angling up at me, fills my eye with ardent color,
and the possibility of, once again, passion.

In the tent: Flathead Lake, Montana

The inner skin of it, white under the yellow fly,
catches the sun like a sail. Like grace, this is
the heat of comfort for a chill body, a soul stiff
with cold. A bright burn, this double flame of nylon,

also, a sack full of sound, a succulent racket in the ear,
a slap and slosh of lake waves, a hollow suck
under the dock. My small tabernacle welcomes sibilance,
sanctions radiance, holds warmth, draws the line at dew.

And rain. Across the lake the black curtain moves,
a threat, a solemnity of storm. But for now no dark drops beat
their blunt staccato on my drum. Only the golden oil of
sunlight anoints me, close as the tent of my own skin.

Windy

The maple seeds have spent themselves;
their wings lie mute and brown and tattered
along the grass. The peonies
have let their bloodied white be scattered,
and all this windy afternoon
I've grieved as if it really mattered.

One

Winter, and very cold,
and the night at
its deepest. The politicians,
as usual, double-tongued.
The town chaotic, teeming
with strangers.
And tonight, as often
in winter, in Bethlehem,
snow is falling.

I always love
how each flake,
torn from the sky,
arrives separately,
without sound, almost
unnoticed in
a flurry of others. How
each one (on a clear
night) lies there glittering
on the swelling breast
of snow, crisp
and intact, as wholly itself
as every radiant star
in a sky sparkling
with galaxies.

How many new
babies tonight
in Judea, coming
like snow flakes?
But plucked,
dazzling, from the
eternal heavens

into time,
tonight is born
The One.

Snow fall

On Riverside Drive
only the sleds move; New Yorkers
are learning to toboggan a slope
on a kayak, a pizza box.

The front page of the *New York Times*
is a blizzard of photos: Times Square
a white desert. Cars, like coffins under
their palls of snow, line 94th Street.
Along Broadway a few pedestrians
lean into the wind, mere smudges
in the camera lens, ignoring
the green yellow red, green yellow red
blinking at non-existent traffic.

Skyscrapers haunt the city—
each tall ghost in its white shroud.
When the air clears—thin
and startling as crystal—
the frozen buildings still gaze at us
with their blank eyes of windows.
In a chilled apartment building
a woman sits, warmed by the soft, white
cat in her lap.

White on black

The monody of cats feuding in the outside stairwell
splits the night between the brick walls.
The sinewy sounds rise—a vortex of wails—
through the cold window behind my headboard, like
a predator dream itching to expose itself,
clawing at my consciousness. I know the why
of my panic: the nightmare of being
shut in a box with this fierce shadow.

Then the white princess, softest of house cats,
cracks the door, insinuates herself almost
without sound, bumps up onto the bed.
Her eyes, lenses of the night, scan
the dim room (as is her habit) for some dusky garment
on which to bequeath her white fur, like a skin
of frost. Instead, she finds me, claims the hollow
of my body for her nest. Like a blotter
I absorb the warmth of paws, the rhythm of
push and pull, familiar as breathing.
Sleep falls kindly as snow, a drift of silk.

When I wake to the faint alarm of sunlight
across the sheets, the ticking clock has crystallized
the air. The cat is gone, having printed
my black sweater on the floor with her
faint shape in white. The way dreams evaporate
with waking. The way the only scrap we keep
is the memory of having dreamed.

Frosty

my winter
breath
is making
small ghosts
out of
night air

unsure of
their shape
they drift
dissolving
in thin
moonlight

leaves of
dark poplars
nod
endlessly
in the wind
rustling yes
yes
keep trying
you've almost
got it

but with lips
stiff as
frozen petals
I give up on
ghosts
try whistling
to turn
my breath
into something
warmer

Weather forecast: Prolonged dry period

The cattle who should, according
to folklore, be lying down at the approach of rain,
stand skeptical in a field of ragged green. The sky,
a surging pewter, exhibits a tatter of gulls.

Like cows, I live under a conditional heaven;
clouds keep tearing apart, then mending,
heavy with partial images. Moments ago
a sheaf of rain, weighted with promise, breached

the foothills. Now its silver ghost
breasts the cow pasture, looms closer, then passes
barely a hundred yards to my left. It
never even blesses my forehead with its fierce

mist. In tune with the random weather,
its errors of judgment, I wait. But what?
A wind from the south? A green
perfection? A seven-year drought?

The forecaster preaches his dogma, predicting
high pressure as long and irritating as intractable optimism.
He may prove wrong. I long to be soaked through.
I want it to pour, relentless, for weeks.

Morning at Legoe Bay

for John, my brother

April 24. Not a day that seemed in any way special,
only a mind marker of the morning we ferried
out to the Island. We watched a new house being framed
to a song of saws and percussion, all yellow pine
and cedar sawdust, a skeleton of possibilities.
At the beach we spread a blue tarpaulin on the rocks
(unyielding, but warm against our bones) and
sanctified the shore by dozing there, in the sun.

Later we wandered, irresolute, loaded our pockets
with stones. I took photos of you, and of the twisted roots
of old logs beached at random angles, oval pebbles
in their elbows and groins where the tide's chaos
had lodged them, like cabochons in free-form
platinum settings. Just days before
you'd told me about the small stone lodged in you,
the clawed cell, visible only on the slides, the scans,
that shadowed every thought, though we laughed absurdly
from time to time. We were watching for signs, but
the little waves in the sun, in the shore's reflection,
danced like a million silver tongues thrusting in and out,
a language we couldn't translate. A sharp wind probed
from the north, and we let the sun search us out
on that day, a day like any other, and like no other.

4

THE DOOR, THE WINDOW

The door, the window

To get older is to watch the door close inch by inch
against my will so that the inflow of silky air
stops, and the creek's subtleties of sound.
In the small house of my ear I listen closely to
the message of blood, knowing others are deaf to it,
as I begin to be to their soft speech across
the dinner table. My memory thins; names drift
just beyond the rim of recollection. I'm told
the floaters in my right eye are only gel thickening
into dark splinters that diminish the light.
"Nothing can be done," my doctor says. "You'll
get used to them." I am not getting used to them.

My years undermine me, eating away in the dark,
silent as carpenter ants in the beams. The pine mirror
in the bathroom reflects my white slackness; why
are my cells failing me just when I am
getting the hang of their glistening life? The minutes
wear me away—a transparent bar of glycerin soap,
a curved amber lozenge dissolving
in daily basins of water. The window glass, brittle
as the scalloped collars of ice that shrink our stream,
still opens its icon eye to me, allows me to see
across the sun-struck grass, white with frost, to hear
the water telling its winter story, telling mine.

Praying and poetry

All week I've been testing
prayers as I hear them coming
from my mouth, judging the slant and
roominess of their pockets, how deep.
How well measured, and
do I take enough time with them.
What about the closeness of their weave,
the hang of fabric, and do they clothe
my gratitude or love or anguish
without bagging or crease.

But never, quite. Nor fit around
his spacious glory. Tailoring
a poem satisfies me better: first
choosing a fabric that goes well
with my skin tones, then all the pinning
and cutting and stitching, the tucking
and tweaking, stripes matching exactly
at the seams, the style planned
to make me look thin and interesting,
showing a selvage of truth, but not
too much, and no frayed edges.

Confession

In your presence, at no great urging from you,
I hold my purse bottom-up over a cascade
of miscellaneous scraps, my self turning inside out
as though my need, too, were bottomless. A tissue
floats to the table. A shopping list and an old
Safeway receipt (food already eaten). A wallet
full of worn green, outgrown photos of my children,
the Washington drivers' license that seems to confirm
my West Coast existence. Saccharin. Tarnished coins
varnished by a thousand sweaty palms. Tablets
to ease heartburn. A scarlet comb tangled with
a disconnection of dark hairs. The keys to house,
car, and only some of the locked doors of my life.
A datebook that foretells the multiple expectations
of the future.
               Inside out, and now the leather interior
is naked as bare skin, seams as ragged as
my worry lines, the emptiness behind
the glossy calfskin and the gold-tone metal: I will
discard. I will purge. I will erase, scour, reverse
a reamed-out heart. See, at last I am
hollow for you. See how I need to be filled.

The holiness of Iona

. . . where two or three gather . . .

Westward across Mull along the
single track, between violet hills and under
the torn cloth of clouds. Finally across
the brief channel from Fionnhport,
the green-gray waves chipping away at the hull
of the ferry, the buffet of sea-wind
rough as the breath of God. Pilgrims,
we three can hardly wait to inhale
the holy island's scent of sanctity.

Arriving, we see the tranquil sea between
the rocks, clear as green glass over the
white sand. Cottage gardens cluster beyond
the jetty, vivid with delphiniums, rank
with nasturtiums. But scores of day-trippers
with back-packs and bikes crowd the asphalt path
to the Abbey; tourists, lacing the air
with foreign syllables, fill the craft shops (local
pottery, celtic jewelry) and the Abbey gift center
(bookmarks, key-rings, post-cards, plastic crosses).

Expecting Columcille and Patrick—
the ancient saints—blessing us with solitude,
with a peace that drops like fading light
behind the hills, all we sense is . . . absence.
Among the shrines and crosses, gravestones,
a nunnery, we each say how we miss it—like
the wild gold of the iris whose dark summer leaves
hug the creases of the island, their spring boldness
faded to a single wilted rag, here, and over there.

On the last day, a walk together across
the close-cropped green velvet and up
over the island backbone of rock to a bay of

pebbles. Then a meal of fish and soda bread,
and evening prayer in the guest room, small
as a cell, showed us where to look, how to see:
Our high anticipation had detoured us away
from God, and holiness, and when we least
expected it, there it was, a felt presence
in our human trinity of longing.

If I only had one hour

what would I get out of it? I used to ask—
What would rush to the top of my thirst
like strings of gold bubbles? But
maybe I wouldn't get. Maybe
I'd give. Cram. Pack the crack in time
with my cells, the colored rags of my best
dreams, my eyes, my open mouth.

Lately I have infinity, and now, like
the aging crescent in the sky, I want to
beam all the gilded light I'll ever see
at drab corners, my face shadowed
by degrees until I am drained of craving,
my self a shrinking balloon—a sack
ready to catch a wing, a grace note, a minim
of stars, whatever comes next.

Madeleine's candlesticks

Zabar's, a New York Saturday morning, I bought
a box of rosy pillar candles, packed
like quadruplets in the womb, for her four

silver candlesticks which stand, flanking
the orange tulips at table center, tall
and elegant as Madeleine herself. Flames

have danced their highlights on the faces
around the oval table ever since
the sterling quartet was willed to her.

Every visit I search the kitchen for
the soft cotton rags and the clay-colored polish
(a favor; her maid "doesn't do silver").

One afternoon, buffing away, I noticed her name
misspelled "Madeline," etched faint
along one oval base. I knew then I was polishing

not just her treasures but my friend, burnishing
with the well-worn cloth of friendship her silver
self, lifting the light tarnish of time and wear.

Like my shining her words into their
places in her books; like her lighting
blooms of fire in a thousand shadowed rooms.

Phone call from the hospital

On the other side of town the phone swings, unhanded.
Here, at the hospital, I hear it knocking that far wall
    clumsily—
its listening ear channels to me the random sounds
of waiting. "I think she's outside, raking," he'd said.

I listen to the hall clock—loud ticking, then twelve discordant
    chimes.
More distantly a Puccini aria springs from some black
    plastic box,
a song of love lost, the music absorbed by air the way the
    hot life
of my coffee is cooling on its way through the porcelain
    handle

to my fingers, the way blood coagulates. I hear him calling
and listen as the faint scritch, scritch of metal on gravel
    pauses,
stops. And now the phone dangles,
plumb-line still, raking in static, the small lint of silence.

The waiting has turned the harsh message into
a clot of words in my throat. Then the faint, blunt rattle
of a screen door opening, the click as it slams,
the slap of sandaled feet running down the hall.

Shore stones

It isn't just that water
wears at the stones
but even small waves
wash things against
each other
ceaselessly,
easing the edges.

Still essentially
our mineral selves,
each of our
colored pebbles
is rounding in the wash
of heaven's waters
and the rub of other
shore stones.

Seating assignment

If you have ever been bumped up
to seat 1A on a 747 you'll know how I feel.
It's been a while since I've been 1A
in anyone's book. It's hard to believe

there hasn't been some kind of mistake.
Sometimes they overbook, I guess—or else why
am I here, with a godlike flight attendant
passing around hot, steaming facecloths,

shaking out the spotless linen cloth
over my tray table, like a robe
of righteousness, and setting down
the tray, with its miniature silver salts

and peppers, the Caesar tossed with
real anchovies, the shining cutlery sheathed
in a napkin (cold as Jesus' head, still
polished and icy from the grave). And free

champagne, its tall flute crystal thin,
its strands of pale gold bubbles ascending
like small thanksgivings to someone who says,
Celebrate! You're worth it! But all of us

airborne strangers on the flight, reclining
in the wide leather seats at 36,000 feet
with heavenly music piped in through the
complimentary headsets—are we really worthy

of this beneficence? Have we earned our way here,
working hard enough to guarantee ourselves
seats up front, a few feet from the pilot?
Did we live right, treating our spouses and our kids

charitably enough to merit this Special Treatment?
The oily look of the character in 1C, the one with

the leer and the gold chains, reeking of Drakkar Noir,
says no, this is ill-gotten. But honestly, I am no extortioner,

just a dogged writer whose poems dream of coming true,
a flawed, faithful servant, a passenger hearing,
with some reservations that will not go away,
Well done. Enter into the joy of First Class.

Some mornings she simply cannot

Some mornings she simply cannot
bring herself to pray. Even so, a prayer
will break through her clenched lips,
announcing the slow drain at her heart.
She will raise her face from its cage of fingers
and gape at the fog that has lain itself down
over the field behind her house like
a dream of erasure. Even the green trees have
lost color. No air breathes. Not a wing of sound
flies back from the highway behind the hill.

And then some midnight, when faith
has quite emptied itself, a familiar loneliness
makes itself at home under her ribs.
A ghost of God? An inkling? She holds
her breath, listens as a small draught
weathers its way through the eaves,
into her ears. The next moment she hears her child
stir in the room down the hall, calling
her name, as if he names her longing and in
that naming, names a kind of answer.

Lewis Avenue: Gray day in spring

I really want to be
drenched in God.

Sometimes
he lets down a small

cloudburst, enough
to leave me wet

and shiny, for about
ten minutes, but mostly

it's just
gray skies up there—

clouds moving
their dull edges

endlessly across
the sky; a drying wind,

and no rain,
Dammit.

To care and not to care

For you, the thought of not caring must feel
light after heavy shadow,
relief after an elephant's foot on the chest.
To not care signals a disconnect:
Care-less. Not simply a kite riding
the breath of air across the field
but free in space, with no silken affection
tugging from the ground.

To care and *not to care*:
to pare away the spiky husk of burden,
and then to relish
the succulent round fruit of love.

Campfire, state park

The smoldering logs
send up their plumes of heat.
Already he has dredged up his
few scrappy grudges—the leftovers
in the refrigerator, the unmade beds.
She says what she's hoarded for
this weekend, an ache rehearscd and
re-rehearsed, laying open her heart
a little—minor surgery, really,
bloody, but unsatisfactory.
She sees it's not much good
cutting deeper.

In the zipped-up tent, after
they've made hot love, their bodies
go slack, cool. There it is exactly: he's
surfeited with skin and other surfaces;
his mining for gold seems like a scratch
in sand with one fingernail. Only his sleep
goes deep, and now that he's sunk in it,
she begins to suture closed her small
incisions, startled only at the sudden
snap: one more charred log falls
apart, settles to embers
in the fire pit.

Winter nights
for Kristin

Your father, when he died,
left this behind, his "head thing"
he called it—a square
of knitted wool, beige, blue,

to tuck around his head
like a small rug. I finger it
now (the stitches like
his body cells, like all

the intricate minutes of his life),
almost the way I fingered it
growing on the needles,
knitting for him a meager defense

against those Illinois nights
in December when he'd wake
with a headache
from the cold. Afterwards

I slept with it hugged
to my chest like a stuffed
animal—a brief blanket for
my heart, a comfort, like him.

The race

In the end death will beat her. Death always
wins, pulling ahead to beat us all, and
the doctors. No matter the new technologies,
the heroic measures, here's the prize:
the inevitable box lid slamming down on the body
with a wooden certainty.

I'm right. In the hospital, death races through the door
into her room, gets to her before the Code Blue team,
before husband, family, chaplain, and Goodbye.
And I'm wrong. God moves more swiftly; from being by her
in her dying, he reaches heaven faster than light,
pulls her in through the door.

St. Teresa speaks to God, "a consuming fire"

How your love burns me
down and down, burns me
down like a candle.

How your holy flame
eats my wick, licks
and swallows my wax,

consumes me to brighten
and perfume the room.
How the fire follows

my thread, hungrily
devours my tallow,
burrows down through

the heart of me
to the final flicker
into thin air, when

a curling filament of smoke
flowers from my charred end
like incense, a prayer.

Daddy

Sailed between
coral reefs at night,
"feeling his way"
in the humid dark.
Clowned for cannibals
in Polynesia. Scorned
safety—the first
white man to cross
one tropic island
unarmed, and survive.

Preached, baptized,
doctored, explored,
loved for twenty years.
Moved back to
what was called
the larger world.
In his late fifties, sired
the two of us,
to our mother's
joy and terror.

Woke every day at four
and prayed his way
around the globe,
his face glowing to God
in the dark.

Taught us to sail,
to skate, to devour poems,
to climb mountains.

In the northern
hemisphere, into
his eighties, chose

the harsh baptism of cold,
spurning overcoats,
hot baths, thrashing
whale-like in any icy tub;
through the doors
we could almost feel
the tidal waves.

With shares
in sugar-cane, stirred four
sweet spoons-ful into
every cup of tea "to keep
the industry alive."
Sprinkled sugar even
on meringue, relishing
the grit between his teeth.

In a characteristic
excess of energy,
always climbed stairs
two at a time.

Spent six weeks
crawling on all fours,
after a fall across
a boat thwart,
before walking
upright again.
Only later, on
the X-rays, acknowledged
his fractured,
mended spine.

Grew into his life for
83 years, until leukemia.
Even his last disease
was energetic,

launching him
in two months into
the new adventure.

A week
before he took off,
wrote a goodbye letter
to all his friends:
"Excited. Feel
like a boy expecting
a birthday bicycle;
can hardly wait.
Wonder—what's
heaven like?"

Then climbed
the steps of air
two at a time.

5

WHAT THE WIND CAN DO

What the wind can do

Twilight. With darkness coming on
through the open door, I am losing more and more
of the gold. From the field next to the barn
fog spreads over the house taut and clean as a bed-sheet,
a blotter. Light still falls from the height
but in particles, the way pollen drops to the hand
under an open sunflower.

Then, like a sigh, the night opens its mouth, breathes.
With fog sliding north on this sled of air, a new dime
of light appears like an offering, a lost coin just found,
over a horizon liquid with trees beginning to sway.
Even the dirt road glistens like a river. Oat fields tilt,
undulate under the kneading air, a Welsh green, the stalks
splinters of moon, the body of night dancing silver.

Layers

Lying here in bed. Feeling my years add up and then
subtract back through decades of sheets and quilts,
like the grave clothes that blanketed my two-year self
shivering for the heat of my mother's arms.
Fragmented early-morning dreams, like scrims, shift

across my brain. A rosy fruit shines,
round and tight, a small, sleek face in a halo of tree.
Leaves shield an apple blemish—a dimpled
portal for decay—the way hair hides a forehead scar.
Around its hidden core of seed and worm-rot

the apple fleshes out and out, blush-cheeked,
white-celled, and sweet. Her arms—no, my mother's
whole warm body—folded like layers
of fleshy material, envelop the family newborn,
my brother, close as her heart, while I wait,

detached for two whole months—a desert of distance,
to be her love again. In their slow vegetable rows
below the orchard, dream cabbages and lettuce
layer themselves around their secret blemishes,
fold over leafing fold. Wakened, I lie motionless

in this familiar grave-bed, trying to be warm,
to be good, to be loved. Waiting to rise.
Knowing it's morning, high time to peel off
the comforter, to shower, come clean, and clothe
in Easter garments my own naked, waiting child.

Benediction: Opening the summer cottage

We stop by the roadside on the way in
to pick daisies, feathered grass heads,
the magenta flame of fireweed.

Unpacking, we settle in for the month:
oiling the squeaky screen door, sweeping up
dead flies and mouse droppings (a mouse

has grown a family in the sofa). Through
opened windows the fields breathe
into the musty bedrooms.

I fill my aunt's old washer—
fly-specked linen and tea towels with
mysterious stains—run the wet cloth

through the mangle, water in little rivers
down my arms all the way out to the line,
and later in the afternoon

I pull the stiff tablecloth out of the sky
to cape a table and scent the kitchen
with its metallic incense.

Sliced tomatoes from the farm stand—
sprinkled with brown sugar, salt, vinegar—
they sluice our tongues with summer juice

at the end of the first day. The wildflowers
in the jam jar say the blessing for us
before supper.

"Create in me a clean heart, O Lord . . ."

Upon arrival from the West Coast to be with friends

From the weather map I know that
rain is falling on the open sea, far out.

The ocean is empty. There is no one to observe
the dark rug of rain that flattens waves,

the roiled surface pricked by drops that
celebrate their arrival from the heights

with such exuberant pirouettes, and a sound like
hands clapping (though no one hears).

What seems so crucial about these small particles
entering their great Mother, like birds home to the nest?

Whether or not we notice, water has always welcomed its own
into the bosom. As you with me.

Flathead Lake, Montana

"Christ plays in ten thousand places"—G. M. Hopkins

Lying here on the short grass, I am
a bowl for sunlight.

Silence. A bee. The *lip* of water
over stones. The *swish* and *slap,* hollow

under the dock. Down-shore
a man sawing wood.

Christ in the sunshine laughing
through the green translucent wings

of maple seeds. A bird
resting its song on two notes.

The blue wall

Open the door labeled WOMEN.
Notice the angles, decorously beige,
the unspectacular straight-edged stalls.
Imagine, hidden inside,
the white vitreous bowls and tanks.
Take in a muted linoleum floor, oval
wash basins and predictable chrome taps,
the wall mirror unremarkable as
our own well-worn reflections in it.
The faint antiseptic odor. Even
the paper towels and the way
we know without thinking how
to spool them down with a push
of the hand, like blank pages.

None of this prepares us for
the one bare blue wall,
a sapphire, a sudden
lake in the desert, unlikely as
a peacock in a flurry of hens,
surprising as a circle of sky
seen at the bottom of a well.

Love, the edge of a wing, lifts
for Josie Bellinger

Even in deep sleep, people
living near the airport hear the planes
taking off all night long

Without cognition, in the dark
when I really need the sleep, I feel
words join themselves together and fly up

Beside my friend's front door lies the huge,
hollowed stone her son found in the Nooksack
and packed home on his back

Last night she was wearing the jade pendant
I brought her last Fall, a dull, bronzed green
thin as a knife blade, an insect wing

Imprints: Lindisfarne

1

Here the slow tongue of sea licks at the English coast,
      glazing the shingle—a shallow tray of pebbles—

with its salt saliva. The road stretching out to Holy Island
      hops with hard rain, drowns in the tide

twice a day as Lindisfarne cuts herself off,
      achieves her separation and retreat.

2

Around the Abbey, wind has eaten the faces of angels, carved
      the columned sandstone to abstraction. In the
            neighbor church

the stained glass is grimed with candle wax,
      old prayers have varnished the arches with their
         incense,

and on the low plant by the door, a snail is pressing its
      wet kiss,
         blessing the green with morning silver.

Enthusiasm: The woods in spring

A dull day. The earth track through the scrim of trees
unrolls like a faded ribbon. But to the left,
to the right, the woods are swollen with life,
sap rising, the earth exploding, bushes bursting with
an extravagant vigor. Green spurts from every
notch and knot, stems take color (having rebelled
at their strict winter uniform of gray); after drinking rain
all winter, canes and brambles, gravid with juice,
garnish the exuberant air with twigs in cinnamon,
snuff, rose, saffron, bronze, chestnut—rampant,
an intricate etching. Even the spaces between are thick
with desire. Light shines from the cells of leaves like
little suns. Under a pewter sky all the green is neon.

A sheaf of pussy willow clutched in my hands seems
to be growing from the ends of my arm bones. My face
glows with reflected colors of leaves. My feet root
in the sod. An illusion? But a small, emerald voice declares
in the undergrowth: "Cut me back? Like you, I'll spring up
from the ground to crowd the air again, irrepressible."

Beachcombing

Suddenly, an awareness: I know, without
knowing how, that in the next minute I'll see

an aqua glint in the sand; the sea glass
sets my agenda. Or a flawless, oval pebble

shining wet at the lip of the tide rising.
Or a volute, its helix unfolding so perfectly

it must have been meant. Maybe a knot
of wood so cleanly itself, so tight in its bleached

whorl of grain, that it is hard to imagine it as
once being part of a tree. It might be

a rock that has held its secret fossil
one hundred thousand years for this moment,

its constant signal subliminal, a tone
humming along time to a tingle in my skull,

a premonition of its sly ambush in
the next few yards; the runnel

of my desire marrying the will of God
in a current so resolute it had to happen.